Baby Shark:
The Childhood Genius of Daymond John

Alfred Cleveland

B·H·U
BETTER HALVES
·UNITED·
PUBLISHING

Better Halves United
South Euclid, Ohio

To order, send $13 to:
BHU Publishing
P.O. Box 21434
South Euclid, Ohio 44121
216-203-1764

www.bhupublishing.com
deaconcleveland@bhupublishing.com

FB: alfredcleveland
IG: @alfredcleveland3

Jacket design by: CleveCo Studios

Contents

To my other mother, Margot John,

and all the great moms out there doing it on their own

"God could not be everywhere,

therefore he made mothers."

~ Jewish proverb

INTRODUCTION

I couldn't have been prouder. While standing in the college registration line, I looked over and saw my friend's picture in one of the textbooks a student was reading. Conferring with the professor concerning possible registration, I asked him if I could borrow one temporarily and sat outside the office looking at the cover. *Good, quality textbook*, I thought. *The real deal.*

When I opened it up and began reading the case study on the kid I grew up in Queens, it blew my mind to actually see him in a college textbook.

Reading the details, I lifted my head up and observed those in the class and wondered if any of them fathomed that in 10 years they'd, too, be making history. *Negatory*, their behavior indicated, as I'm sure my pal's did when he found himself at a crossroad sitting on a backstreet curb after a night gone bad with rowdy friends in Times Square. After all, who could really know if greatness lied in their future?

I would love to tell you there was a difference here, with this child of the textbook, that he knew he would one day be assigned by the former leader of the free world to be an ambassador for his Global Entrepreneurialship Initiative. But as sure as you're seeing the ink on this paper, I tell you, absolutely not. The choices, the risks, the haphazardness sometimes displayed in the life of the young Daymond John revealed the fact that he saw himself not much above average. Be that as it may, i will say I have seen glimpses of greatness in him personally that I'd only read about in the lives of other great, young, thinkers of the past like Thomas Edison and Garrett Morgan...the geniuses.

These glimpses are what this book is about and are what these parents need to identify and see. Not the intellect you passed down genetically to your ever-so-gifted child that makes him "sooooo smart," as you told your friends of your child's brilliance. But the moments of genius you spot that need to be developed, harnessed and made better, because smarts doesn't equal greatness.

One approach to this great "spotting" is careful observation. We all need to observe more, like, super closely, what our children have a knack for. This was the pandemic's silver lining for many parents as it allowed time for them to observe more and see things in their children they never saw. Observation alone would be moot, however, if objects then aren't consciously placed in the immediate vicinity of the child to see what they gravitate towards. Maybe it's a paintbrush and paint, perhaps it's placing a Xylophone in the crib. Could be a book or something along the lines of what we could imagine Mr. Manning Sr. placed in his son's Peyton and Eli's hands when they were children.

Once their inclinations are spotted, the harnessing should begin—the training, the lessons, the cultivation of their potential. When a love for that develops, the course has been set toward success. Then you have *purpose*. Raising a child on purpose. With purpose. Ohhhh...now we're encroaching that sacred area—that area of greatness indeed.

Take Richard Williams, the man who persuaded a woman he was no longer in a relationship with, to have two more daughters for the sole purpose of raising them to dominate the world of tennis. Or Tiger Woods, whose father had him on the greens before he was able to walk, then walked him to the top of the golf world. But much time need not be spent on these honorable mentions of great achievement when we could go directly to the head honcho of purpose and greatness, Jesus Himself. Who lived with greater purpose than He?

While in the womb His virgin mother was told who He was and of His very mission, and therefore had the advantage of raising Him on purpose. Every action, every word, every jot, every tittle, had a purpose. Fortunately, she had a heads-up that her child would be ushered to heights imaginable. But you, dear parent, do you know who you have been given?

The ancients understood very clearly that children were a heritage from God, and that their marriage was a "bank" into which He deposited precious children, who were His investment for the future. Understanding who our children are, that they are rewards and opportunities, as opposed to punishments and obstacles, is the first step to raising the child on purpose. Great wisdom from on high is not required to begin this either. We start, simply, by being examples.

This is what this ingenious child in whom I write about had

growing up. Interestingly enough, it wasn't through the example of a man that he followed either, but of a woman, his dear mother, Margot John.

You'll read book after book, and see episode upon episode of the prodigious shark displaying his business acumen on ABC's Shark Tank. What you don't see, however, is the power of this single mother, with a watchful eye and attentive ear, who raised the young man with such purpose in their modest home in Queens.

Soft-spoken, beautiful, and blessed with a quiet spirit, Ms. John used her skills at a neighborhood salon to send her son to a parochial school with hopes that he'd receive an exceptional education. Underneath the quality of humility, lied a sternness that her child, myself and the rest of his friends respected and loved. Never having to raise her voice, the graciousness of the young mother made them want to do right. That grace, dear mothers, is a gift all women should strive to attain. It is power. I tell you, power.

Daymond's success was not by mistake. It was this healthy respect for grace that produced in him, a fear. Not fear of punishment or wrath for wrongdoing, but fear of letting her down. Though he worked 9-to5 daily, which gave her son ample time after school for adventure and youthful mischievousness, she was a presence in his life.

I can't say enough for presence.

So when you see Mr. John negotiating tough deals, or on talk shows dispersing power points for success in his direct, no-nonsense style, know that you are seeing the product of a child raised under the power of grace.

The Childhood Genius of Daymond John

While I can assure you, unequivocally, that his mother's graciousness was the most potent influence guiding Daymond's life, you will find in these pages stories, lessons, and insights from his life that will work to help you discover the greatness and genius in your own child's life amidst the normalcy, that could unlock their potential and guide them to success in their own right.

These are the childhood experiences of Daymond John, the brand guru, fashion mogul and investor you've come to know...and his adventures with a friend who's been rooting for him the whole way. Welcome to the backstory of a true American hero.

CHAPTER ONE

The Beehive

The more members, the more producers, was the thought behind having large families in America at one time. Small communities thrived from the agricultural households of our nation's heartland. But in the midst of widespread growth in the late 1800's, something began to happen to the family structure that started ripping at its fabric.

The security, economic and social status in communities that large families once beheld, slowly began to dissipate as younger members broke off and sought work in the factory-laden cities in the north. In these cities a new family structure began to take shape into what we now call the Nuclear family—man, woman, and perhaps a child or two.

As a result of President Lyndon B. Johnson's lenient immigration laws of 1965, immigrants from around the world began entering the US workforce, competing with the now, smaller families.

During this time, Queens, New York, had become a hub for these fine mixtures of families in search of prosperity and the limitless opportunities the US provided. With warehouses, factories, subways, and various transportation opportunities abounding next door to a booming island called Manhattan, purchased from the Indians in 1626 for $24, Queens became the perfect place of refuge, just affordable and far away enough from the city to raise a family in search of the new American dream.

Around the same time, Garfield John Sr., as a teenager, left his home in Trinidad all by himself and headed for New York in the same pursuit.

Once arriving there, the adventurous and highly motivated man began working menial jobs until he worked his way up as a computer programmer on those huge, slow-moving computers of the 70's. He rented a room out in the home of Margot's parents and a few years later the young Margot gave birth to the baby shark, Garfield Daymond John.

With a plan to raise a family together, the two bought a house on the border of Hollis and St. Albans, Queens, a community they found perfect to achieve this goal. Named after a converted Roman soldier beheaded in one of England's small towns, St. Albans became the foreign country's first Christian martyr. Beloved by the church and his countrymen, St. Albans was given sainthood and a small city there was named after him. Following suit, the founding fathers of New York named one of its suburbs after the patron saint to attract European settlers to the virgin territory in order to further economic growth, where centuries later, families began migrating from all over the world to climb its social ladder.

Turns out, St. Albans and Hollis became predominantly African-American, but the area surrounding it embodied the spirit of New York's melting pot becoming home to many Puerto Rican, Dominican, Jamaican, Asian, African-American, and white families, all working-class folks, trying to get ahead.

Finally established as a family in the small community, to her dismay, Margot soon discovered that the man of her dreams was not who he appeared to be, and she refused to put up with his many lies, infidelities, and excuses. With complete unrest in the house, the Trinidadian native moved out and Margot filed for divorce. Their son was 10 years old.

The split, however, didn't stop the young mother's determination to groom her son into the man she knew he'd become.

Strategically placed in a prime location, she rented a small nail booth in a beauty salon right in front of the suburb's primary shopping district, one that also sat directly across from the borough's busiest bus terminal on Jamaica Avenue. If you were from Hollis, Hollis Hills, Laurelton, Jamaica, Jamaica Estates, the South Side, or St. Albans, chances are, if you worked or went to school in Queens, you passed through this hub daily.

Made famous to the world by the renowned rap group, Run-DMC, "The Ave," as what it would come to be known as, was a five-block stretch of jewelry, music, electronics, clothes, and shoe stores along Jamaica Avenue that sat in the heart of the borough. Oftentimes, Daymond would be summonsed by his mother to the salon to get money to pay a phone or electric bill, or perhaps run an errand. On many occasions, while he sat in the waiting area, he could be found gazing across the street at the lines of pedestrians in the packed bus terminal or out the front window at the shoppers who walked by with bags of clothes and boxes of shoes. The careful observer he was, he'd turn his attention back into the shop where he'd listen to the background chatter of the women in the busy salon while watching his mother render nail care services to the beautiful working ladies of Queens. He took it all in.

From her example, it was here that he learned one of the earliest unspoken lessons of business that could take one years to learn in a university without, perhaps, fully grasping its importance. It was crystal clear to the boy that the success of a business relied heavily on its Location. Business gurus of old have long preached about this key principle in books, videos and seminars, with chants such as Location, Location, Location! But sitting quietly in a salon, the young Daymond recognized by simple observation that prime real estate was crucial to the success of any business, and this place was a beehive.

4

CHAPTER TWO
Seeds of a Fashion Empire

Margo wanted her son to have the education she never had so she worked daily, going the extra mile for her customers to send her son to the neighborhood catholic school, St. Gerard's Majella.

In attendance at the school were children from nationalities around the world, and it was here that Daymond gained a healthy knowledge and respect for various cultures, which would lay the foundation years later for his comfortability in traveling in other countries. Nancy from China, Giselle from Portugal, Richard from the Dominican Republic, Robert from Mexico, Stacey from the Philippines, Edward from the West Indies, Rudy from Africa, the Rivera Twins from Ecuador, Gustavo from Cuba, and me from the hood.

There was much wisdom to Margo John's decision to invest in Daymond's future by sending him to the school she'd have to pay for rather than the four other schools in the area. Notwithstanding the catholic school's reputation for scholastic discipline and teaching of biblical ethics, the school's attire proved to be a very attractive selling point. Dress shirts and ties, overlaid with nice-looking burgundy sweaters and grey slacks to match, shoes were a must-wear with the school's uniform. This to the mother, was preparing her son for the professional waters she knew he'd one day swim. "Futures can not be chosen," she said. "But habits could. And its your habits that choose your future."

For many years to come, this school would serve as the base for many adventurous journeys, life-long relationships, a plethora of life lessons, and yes, mischief.

Just a mile or so away, was his home. Mine was a little further down the road, but both seemed like other worlds compared to life at school. We lived on the other side of the tracks, literally, where the cultural diversity of our school's area turned all black. It was here that our other set of friends went to schools known to be a little rougher than what we were comfortable with. We'd heard the countless stories of group fights, occasional stabbings, and kids who outright disrespected the teachers—behavior that wasn't even conceivable with the nuns. Their square, pilgrim-like shoes with the buckle, for some reason conveyed the message that one would be swift-kicked in a heartbeat, while the outside portrayed purity and serenity. But I was no fool. Howbeit, the contrast worked wonders on the mind.

The bloody red wooden paddle on the principle's wall with Latin words inscribed in the meat of it left us bewildered as to what it meant, but signified to all the students that the beating would be Christ-like for those that got out of line. The glaring difference between our school life and that of our neighborhood made us feel like we were both living double lives. Ones that we liked. It seemed to be the best of both worlds.

6

Quarterly, our school hosted a dance, which was an opportunity for us to let our hair down and wear street clothes. This presented a chance for us to show our individuality and unique styles. This also gave Daymond, Sammy, Thomas, Richard, and I a chance to show our solidarity as a break-dance and graffiti crew. We were all fairly decent artists and dancers, but none of our skills, dancing abilities, or coolness matched up to Don Cotton's, a handsome Latino break-dancer with lots of swag.

He lived in the school's area, but none of us ever knew how he managed to get in the school dances every time. We all envied him, for various reasons, but primarily because he always stole all the girls' attention. This guy was the spanish Fonz. Minus him, we were the man, plural.

To compete with this fellow, we knew we had to step our gear up, so we'd take a trip before the dance to Mr. Lee's Sweatshop on The Ave to design our crew's shirts. We were T.W.C., *The Wonder Crew*, allegedly for the wondrous moves we'd create when we would break-dance and pop-lock. But word got to us that Don's interpretation for T.W.C. stood for something else—The Wonder Bread Crew, after the nearby bread factory. We all understood and resented the implication, but none of us really wanted trouble with this cool street kid. We would outshine him though.

With designs, color schemes, and money we'd been saving for weeks in hand, Daymond and I, who seemed to be the crew's designers, would make the trip up to Mr. Lee's to have our sweatshirts made for the dance.

"What letter do like," Mr. Lee would ask, referring to the various fonts and designs he had in his book. Picking the

7

right letters were crucial. We were graffiti artists after all, the lettering had to be tight.

After picking out the sweatshirt's color for that season, we'd lay the first one down on the glass table-top and begin the outlay of the letters, placing our crew name in a circle on the front, our names on the sleeves and any number of things on the back, usually a pre-designed iron-on zodiac sign. Then the lightning bolts and extra iron-on cut-outs would be strategically placed on the sweatshirt for emphasis.

Once complete, Mr. Lee's assistant daughter would lay the sweatshirt on the flat iron to seal our name in break-dance crew infamy.

Yeeeaah, we'd be thinking as we glanced at each other, seeing the finished product get lifted off. *We'll show him.*

In the early 80's, there were no African-American clothing designers. Women wore Jordache if they could afford them and the guys with a few bucks wore Lee Denims. Some rocked Levi's or Devils, remember those? If you could buy some Fila, Pumas, or Shell-toes, you were that dude. An Adidas suit or leather jacket? Other level.

A new generation was emerging, however. A culture of youth with a desire to express themselves and their individuality in a unique way. Before Cross Colours, Damage Jeans, Karl Kani, or any other African-American designers hit the scene, a deep yearning was present and emerging in the hip-hop world through this visionary kid designer who used what he had at the time to make his own shirts. Before the college textbook stories of Daymond's fashion beginnings with hand-made hats, the seeds of self-expression were being birthed on little sweatshirts through which an idea would form into an iconic clothing line that would soon change the world. The spirit of Hip-Hop was pushing its disciples to the surface of notoriety...and him to independence. Before the thought of FUBU was ever conceived, a vacuum of need was brewing in the soul of the culture, and fate was tugging at the heart of its creative leader. Forward...

CHAPTER THREE
The Burning Barn

Like Lewis and Clark, the famous explorers taught to us by our 3rd grade teacher Ms. Gallagher, who were commissioned by Thomas Jefferson in 1803 to find a traveling route west through the Continental Divide, or Ponce de Leone, the ruthless explorer from Spain who conquered Puerto Rico in 1508, or even the astronauts Neil Armstrong and John Glenn who traveled to the moon, Daymond and I wanted so badly to be like these historical figures on their adventurous journeys. Unlike our super-bright student counterparts who could rattle off mathematical formulas and elements from the Periodic Table at a moments notice, neither Daymond or I cared very much for the complex components of education. But we did love Social Studies and its many explorers.

Much like the brave men we idolized and read about in the history books, after school Daymond and I would set out on expeditions of our own.

On some of our more risky excursions, we'd travel to swampy areas the opposite way from home to catch crickets and grasshoppers for our turtles, or would go hiking through

Cunningham Park's wilderness. The winding, dirt trails of the park on the other side of the Grand Central Parkway were long and many, so much so that one could easily get lost. But somehow, we always managed to find our way out. We loved nature and the outdoors. But this was the closest we could come to it at the time in our New York lives.

Deep in the park, however, we would often run into motocross riders who would dangerously roll over logs and emerge from dirt valleys at high speeds, launching themselves high into the air on their bikes. Wherever we were going, when we stumbled upon this exciting and hidden place in the park, we were always mesmerized by the stunts and roars of the motorcycles. We'd watch and watch until it seemed every time the event's finale would arrive.

Cuddled away in the park was a Highway Patrol station where State Troopers would emerge onto the nearby Grand Central Parkway to catch speeding motorists and other bad guys. But they had another division of lawbreakers they set out to catch. The Motocrossers.

The greatest part of the event was seeing the Highway Patrol dirt-bike unit sneak up on the riders and chase them through the park. What fun it was to sit front row seat to our very own police chase. This is where the talents of the real motocross riders shined, doing dangerous things the cops would never do. And as always, they always got away!

Though we dreamed of one day having the courage to ride dirt-bike motorcycles and do some of the tricks we saw the riders do, we stayed true to the semi-dangerous feats of jumping ramps and speeding down twisting, obstacle-

12

laden trails on our bicycles. We loved the adrenaline and excitement of watching the motorcyclists, but we weren't willing to take such dangerous risks that could cause serious or permanent damage to one's limbs or skull.

This is a behavior that would serve Daymond well in the future as a disciplined investor. He is willing to take risks in business, and one must be if one wants to take his company to higher levels, but dangerous risks were, back then, as they are for him now, out of the question. His were always calculated and well thought our. He always counted the costs.

On most days, however, our journeys would take place on the way home, where our first stop after school would be Elman's Convenient store. It was here that we'd stock up on Pez candies, Blow Pops, Twinkies, and Quarter Water drinks. We needed to fuel up for the trek ahead.

Our next stop was the McDonald's across the street, but our intentions there were not for the Mac and fries. Behind the restaurant sat its parking lot over which sat tall walls and poles that lit up the lot at night. Towering over and behind the parking lot, sat the Woodhull Apartments, a block-long string of buildings that one had to enter from around the corner. After going around and through the apartment building's entrance as if we lived there, we'd come out through a fire exit high on the roof overlooking the McDonald's parking lot, except now we were towering over it five stories high.

Leaning over the edge by the pole that extended up past us, we'd look down at the cars and customers going in and out until the time was right. Then, like brave astronauts with our backpack "air-supply tanks" on, we'd climb upon the ledge and jump, taking "One giant leap for mankind" onto the pole, bear-hugging it as we slid down top-speed to the parking lot ground. Then back around and up and down we'd go, until, almost religiously about our third round, the heavy-set, slow running manager with a huge head we called, "The Cat in the Hat," would come out and chase us away—right onto the trail of our next expedition, The Burning Barn.

The only thing that separated the railroad tracks from the backyard of this abandoned house was an old fence and the foliage of a few bushes. It was in this backyard that a semi-burnt garage sat, filled with rusty bike frames and old car parts that we came to play in.

Making our way up its driveway past the dilapidated house, we'd always look at the graffiti-riddled boards nailed over the windows and doorway that said, Keep Out!" But looking is as close we'd ever go to the house. We got the message.

Once in the backyard, we'd kick the old tires filled with rain water to awaken the sleeping mosquito larvae we called, "Tadpoles" and watched them wiggle around a little bit. After a few minutes of examining our pet specimens, we'd march over and stomp on the roof of an abandoned car the thieves stripped and left there. This worked to help rid ourselves of some of the youthful aggression we had within. I think every boy needs something to destroy every now and then.

Once that was out of our system, we'd make our way over to the barn for the main event. In front of the garage door sat two mattresses we stacked together and test jumped on to check its bouncibility and dryness if it rained. The garage's upper level contained a front window, well...a hole where a window once sat, that served as the exit door of our "Army plane."

Making our way through spider webs, over dirty pipes, corroded wood, and broken down baby carriages, we climbed the wooden ladder to the garage's upper level. Walking around a musty couch no-one would dare think of sitting on, we stood by the front opening to look at the ghetto trampoline, which now looked to be miles down. Every time was like the first time, and our hearts raced as we prepared to make another jump for the day, this time out our B-52 bomber.

After a moment of contemplation, which was more like a silent prayer, I'd always make the jump first. I had no problem with it as I tightened my knapsack "parachute" straps and jumped out the hatch onto the mattresses, which in classic Ninja style we'd roll over and onto our feet in enemy territory. For added effect, our school uniforms gave the impression we were much heralded Navy Seals on a heroic mission to save the world. That's how we felt. And still do.

CHAPTER FOUR
Young Businessmen

Daymond's house was the next stop. Once there, his first order of business was to review the instructions his mother left him on the counter of chores he was to complete and food she suggested he'd make.

Before any further play ensued with me or his neighboring friends, Ms. John insisted that all the tasks she outlined for him be complete by the time she got home. A strict disciplinarian she wasn't, but she often followed through on her requests by checking the bathroom, the toilets, the dishes, the carpet for vacuuming, or whatever other chores she asked him to do to see if they were actually done, and done with care. Even on days when he and I had further plans to continue our journey elsewhere, he was disciplined enough to complete his tasks fully before we went anywhere.

Too often, particularly in these days and times, young generations fall victim to the temptation of instant gratification—wanting things they want, when they want it, and wanting them now. Everything in society feeds this monstrous desire, as it profits off the quick-serve, fast-moving microwave generation of today. But if we teach our

17

children to delay their gratification, to work and sacrifice first before the pay-off, they may begin to understand the importance of sowing, then reaping in due time in the cycles of life. Do your children complete their homework first, then go out and play? Or do they have fun first, then come inside to do their homework?

Delaying our pleasures is an important discipline to teach our children and is tantamount to their success, particularly in the business world. Ms. John understood that to give her son chores to complete first, she was not only teaching him patience and discipline, but giving him responsibilities. And if one can show himself faithful in little ones, he can be trusted to be faithful over bigger ones. Daymond was being prepared for bigger through small responsibilities.

Equally of particular interest at the John resident after school, was when young Daymond would cook his meals after one of our expeditions. Notably, two of his favorite after-school meals to whip up were grilled-cheese or egg sandwiches. As simple as these snacks were to make, he had a particular way he seasoned the food and flavored the bread that made the sandwiches quite tasty. This kid had blessed hands. Rachel Ray could take a pointer or two from him.

After flattening the bread with a spatula in the frying pan and flipping the sandwiches over for the last stage of the process, he would not bat an eye in indicating he was going to offer me any. So I'd ask.

"Whassup," I'd mutter. "The usual?"

"How many?" he'd respond, still cooking. "Two."

18

"That's it?"

"And something to drink."

We had been through this routine tens of times, but in an attempt to at least make him feel bad, I'd ask him "How much?"

"Fifty-cents," he'd reply, never budging from his asking price.

"Each?" as if I was outraged, every time.

"And a quarter for the punch," he would add. This guy was brutal.

I often wondered if he did this to anyone else or just me because he knew I had it, but I would, as time went on, find out that that's just what young businessmen did. But coughing up the $1.25 was something I did every time, as I truly enjoyed the meals.

Flashes of hidden business talents like these, which may only be detected by the closely observant eye, should be looked out for by all parents. The problem in our society is, America focuses its attention primarily on those who are talented in the areas of athletics, song, dance, art, or craftsmanship, while less attention is placed on the innovators, the academians, the intellectual athletes, and the businessmen.

As a man born in Africa may never discover his true talents as a hockey player because of its hot weather, our country's focus, it seems, is fixated on the obvious talents, devaluing the strength and power of the majority who possess

19

powerful, yet subtle talents. We are just now beginning to discover these brilliant minds as technology increases and more young geniuses are changing the world through their ideas. If you discover your child has leadership qualities, or an affinity for business, do not brush it off. There are now schools, courses, books, DVD's, and programs you can enroll him/her in that will harness their leadership giftings.

Watch your children's strengths and abilities closely, not for what you want them to be, but for what they are. Then invest in developing them.

20

CHAPTER FIVE

The Glass Company

The astuteness of the baby shark didn't stop at the sandwiches he sold in his kitchen, but expanded far beyond the home.

On the last leg of our journey from school before we made it to his house where we ate, we'd walk by a factory at the end of a string of small warehouses a few blocks away. They made mirror items for the home and businesses, and expensive glass chess and backgammon boards. We called it The Glass Company.

Outside the small factory sat a commercial dumpster where they disposed of broken mirrors and negative pieces they cut off from mirror products they made. Rectangles, squares, circles, and triangles in divers sizes were thrown into the bin daily by its workers.

While walking home, we'd innocently stroll by the open factory, cutting our eyes into the huge trash-bin to see if it was full, but never breaking a stride. If it was full, that meant the dumpster would remain unlocked for the night so the commercial sanitation truck could pick it up in the morning. For us, this meant, tonight was the night to strike.

Making sure all my homework was done quickly, I'd set out back to Daymond's as the sun was going down where he'd be anxiously waiting with his hoodie and gloves on.

"Here," he'd say, handing me the extra pair of thick multi-purpose gloves, and we'd transform from saints to sinners.

Our window of opportunity sat between the time the factory closed at 5 and before it got dark at 6. We needed to see what we were doing. With the place deserted and just enough sun left for a good rummage, we climbed atop the green monster and with all our strength tossed over the lid to reveal the dumpster's treasures.

On a good day, we'd come out with a paper bag full of mirrors each, but we paid the price in blood as our hands would sometimes get scratched and cut through the gloves from the sharp edges of the glass. We'd stay digging until just before it got dark or until we heard the Supersonic Concorde flying by to the airport. Daymond's curfew was earlier than mine and the plane was his nightly cue to be home.

When he heard it he'd instantly wrap it up and start heading home for the 5-minute walk.

"Hey! You need to help me close this lid!" I'd shout.

He would then come back, help me, then peel out with jewels in tow.

These spoils turned into a pocketful of coins the next morning as we'd be on the schoolyard early before the school doors opened peddling mirrors to our kid colleagues. They'd use the mirrors for all kinds of things. The girls loved the circle and rectangle ones to brush their hair and do makeup with, while the boys loved the thin strips for their rooms. Nameplates and belt-buckles with one's name on it was the popular thing back then, so gluing one's name on his room wall with the mirrors was the next coolest thing going. They'd get the other shapes for added decoration, and we couldn't keep enough of them.

We always kept a few palm-sized pieces for ourselves, however, for less honorable purposes unfortunately. Definitely not to glue on a wall.

During recess, one could find us in the classroom, lunchroom, or playground talking to the girls and laughing. We would mount small mirrors in our shoelaces to look under the girl's dresses. We couldn't really see anything except a panty color, but it sure was fun thinking we could!

When the girls discovered what we were doing they'd laugh and chase us away. But as time went on, we got beside ourselves with one girl and surpassed the voyeurism. We started squeezing her butt. We thought she liked it because she would giggle and let us do it for weeks, but I think we became annoying. We found out how much so when she told her parents and we found ourselves in Sister Helen's office.

We were both grounded for weeks and ordered straight home after school, which crippled our $40-a-week business. In all actuality this was good for us, because we had a problem. And this problem, unfortunately turned into a bad habit. A habit that we both managed to keep

23

secret from everyone—one that got so bad it turned into an addiction that had us spending all our hard-earned profits on daily. The spot we did it in was Mr. Juan's, a small diner by our school with a dark back room...with one video game. Donkey Kong was our drug!

When our sentence was lifted and our better-come-straight-home-from-school directive was removed, our expeditions and business venture resumed and thrived more than ever! The kids couldn't wait to get more mirrors! This became our first lesson in one of business' most important principles: the power of Supply and Demand. Flood the market. Stop. Make 'em hungry for it. Then hit 'em again. Daymond even raised his prices on sizes I didn't have. Shrewd. He understood the power of the principle thoroughly.

And oh yeah, we wised-up and stopped using the mirrors for evil. Don't judge us!

CHAPTER SIX
Product Envy

Our love for outdoors grew stronger and stronger as we would go camping in Connecticut with our partner Sammy and his mother. These camping trips meant the world to us, as now our expeditions would be taken to a new level. And the fact that Sam's mom was a shapely Army Sergeant by occupation, made the trip all that more enjoyable for us young lads.

Every morning at the campgrounds, Daymond and I would wake up long before sunrise and exit the camper to prepare our fishing poles and tackle-boxes for the much anticipated day on the lake. Oh, how we loved to fish! This was another valuable quality Daymond had—*Alacrity*, which in the Webster's Dictionary is defined as Cheerful eagerness.

When one begins to love a thing, it will usually produce that cheerful eagerness in the person that will drive them to learn as much about the thing as possible. In other words, passion! This passion will produce a host of other good traits too, like rising up early in the morning and arriving early before appointments. Anything that Daymond developed a love for, you could rely upon him to be there promptly. On nights that we made plans to hit the Glass Company, he was always on time and waiting. And it was this reliability that helped him to be the businessman he is today, which is a hallmark of successful people around the globe. Good businessmen don't have to be dependable, but great ones are.

If Sammy didn't wake up, he'd just miss the trip. But we didn't care, nor did we get much sleep on those nights.

At dawn, while the fog was still rolling in off the lake, we'd be at the bank digging for bait. We both had an eye for picking the plump, juicy worms that we knew would drive the fish crazy, and we always found plenty of them. Plus, Sam's mom would give us bread and kernels of corn that also drove our underwater friends crazy.

As we rowed out to find a spot we thought the fish would be biting, we'd throw the anchor overboard and get to work. Daymond and I were both exceptionally good fishermen even when we fished other places with grown men. I think this was so because I believe we both had the ability to think like fish. Plus we read boyscout and other outdoor magazines all the time and learned simple tips like the importance of washing our hands. Gasoline, oil from cars, and other household smells repel fish because some of these products hold the same odor their underwater enemies produce. Other smells from chemicals had the same effect. It was this kind of love and seriousness we had for the event that resulted in our buckets being filled with fish at the end of the day.

Thinking like fish was a honed gift that, today, still allows him to know what consumers want. The key is, like worms, if something appealed to him (a vessel he feels represents the likes of millions of people), then he knew it would appeal to a mass number of others. In this case, if the worm looked plump and juicy to him, then he knew it would be very attractive to the fish. Same with products. He knows that if he likes it, millions of others will too. And his gift hasn't proven him wrong yet!

"Oh...great job," Sam's mom would tell us, as she took the bucket, cleaned the fish, and prepared dinner for us. As we ate the cornmeal-battered fish that absolutely melted in our mouths, with creamy corn and cheese Broccoli on the side, we were in heaven partaking in our kill, and watching her boobs.

In many service occupations such as teachers, ministers, and those that work in homeless shelters etc., there is a dilemma that plagues these providers called "Product Envy."

A man who owns a factory can determine his profits by how many widgets he produced throughout the day what his profits will be at the end of the day. In other words, he can see the immediate results of his labor. Those in the service sector who work to help people, don't often see the fruits of their labor in the lives of people, which, oftentimes, makes the service worker grow weary and envious of the businessman.

While Daymond always had a big heart to help people, as an altar boy for many years, he could have very well traveled down the road of ministry. But the pleasures he received from the likes of fishing and being able to, at the end of the day, reap the rewards of his labor, his calling to business

27

was evident. Business is what he was built for, though he still serves in a unique way by investing in people, and teaching them to fish, metaphorically.

CHAPTER SEVEN
Ranger Rick

For more fun at the campgrounds, there were other activities we loved, one of which took place under a huge tent on Saturday nights. We weren't under that tent, but we'd watch the folks there for hours, gather, drink moonshine, and square dance to high-tempo Country-western music all through the night.

Being the only blacks on the entire campground, we made sure we kept our distance as they danced and partied, and just observed these peculiar folks from the dark woods. We wanted to see them undisturbed in their own element, enjoying themselves and having fun to this "rodeo music," as we called it. We loved other people's cultures.

Once we became bored, it seemed like a good idea for us to get some undisturbed time at the main area where the showers and laundry room were. We discovered a day earlier they had video-games in the back.

Centipede and, whaddayaknow, Donkey Kong! Problem was, we only had a few quarters combined, so when we ran out, we stood there looking at each other like idiots...maybe more like fiends.

Suddenly, a screwdriver flicked out from Daymond's pocket-knife and him and Sammy began prying open the Centipede's coin box. Having moved a little too quick, I got nervous and moved towards the door. When I got there my heart skipped a beat when I saw Ranger Rick ride by on his ATV.

Ranger Rick was the campground's lawman, a short, slender, well-built old man who wore a buttoned-down corduroy shirt, jeans, cowboy boots, and a cowboy hat. I don't know if he was a real Ranger, but as far as I was concerned that cowboy hat made him Sheriff around these parts.

By the time I eased back where the other two were, they were already dividing coins and deciding who was going to play next. That quick. I told you we were addicts!

"Ranger Rick just rode by!" I whispered, skittishly.

"Which way'd he go?" Sammy asked. Sammy had been camping there with his mother for years and Ranger Rick knew him. But Daymond wasn't worried at all, a little too nonchalant for my liking. He didn't realize that we now had to make it all the way back to our camper without being seen, because if anyone saw us in that vicinity they'd have good cause to suspect we were the culprits. How so, you might ask? Well genius, we were the only black kids on the entire campsite, and the only campers not at the Square Dance. Okay, maybe I'm guilty for stereotyping us, but that alone was enough circumstantial evidence to get a conviction for me. Furthermore, we were the bandits!

For some reason, as we dipped in the woods under the cloak of darkness, something possessed Ranger Rick to roll by, park, and walk into the laundry building of all places. We took off running into the thick of the woods until we were deep enough to use our flashlights and raced towards the camper. The run seemed like forever. In the distance, we could hear the Ranger's ATV racing around the campgrounds, even cruising by our camping area. My gut was telling me Ranger Rick knew it was us.

Being as though it was Saturday and we weren't scheduled to leave until Monday, before Ranger Rick could conduct a thorough investigation I played sick so Sam's mother could take us back to New York.

As we packed up and hitched the camper to the car, we headed toward the exit that Sunday morning where Ranger Rick was sitting on his ATV carving an apple.

"Good day, Ranger," Sam's mother said, as she crawled at a snail's pace past the exit. Flipping a piece into his mouth, he just tipped his hat in return, with his eyes on Daymond and me in the backseat.

Until we hit the state line on the highway, I still felt like we were going to get pulled over. But my anxiety began to subside when we finally did, at which time I looked over at my friend who was napping peacefully with his mouth propped open like he didn't have a care in the world. I knew right then that something was seriously wrong—just didn't know what.

31

CHAPTER EIGHT
The Suffering

Mr. Hensland was a heavy-bearded, dark-haired man with a pale complexion and a bodily shape like Whimpy from Popeye. As gifted a Social Studies teacher he was, making history come alive for us every day, he had an equally hot temper.

As the weeks went on in our new school year, it became apparent that his buttons could be pushed, but of course, nobody would attempt to do so.

For fun, when we were bored in class, Daymond and I had a game we'd play, or rather, he'd play. Since he knew I had plenty of change from our business venture, the game was basically to swindle me out of cash.

Out of our whole crew of break-dancers and graffiti artists, he was the best dancer, but the least talented artist of us all. His drawings were so unsightly, the weirdness of his sketches gave them a strikingly unique quality that actually made them quite brilliant. So much so, they had an ability to make people laugh. So he formed a game with us in which he would bet us a quarter that he could make us laugh.

33

We usually played the game at his house after we'd eat, but today I alone was his target. Plus, he didn't like Mr. Hensland because of his bad attitude and the fact that he always singled him out, so out of boredom he decided he wanted to play.

This particular afternoon, while the summer breeze blew pleasantly through the wide-open window of the quiet class, a note popped up on my desk from behind me. I knew the handwriting, so I glimpsed back across the room to him grinning and nodding his head. Open it, was the gesture.

Inside was the .25 cent challenge. I knew he had the ability, but because of Mr. Hensland's temperament, and my father's included if I got in trouble, I felt I had the willpower to refrain from any outburst, so I wrote back, *No...50 cent.* When he received the note back he smiled and wasted no time going to work. *Money in the bag,* I thought. Little did we know, Mr. Hensland was peeking over the pages of his book.

When the note made its way back to me, I looked back to a big smile and him pretending to be doing schoolwork. I opened it to yet another tried-and-true rendition of Medusa, his usual ace-in-the-hole sketch, and the pure wretchedness of the drawing provoked an outburst of laughter from me in the deafening silent room.

All attention now on me of course, a red-hot Mr. Hensland rushed over and snatched the note from me. He knew it was Daymond's handiwork, and while multiple obscenities flew from his mouth frightening all the students, his exclamation point was flinging his book across the room, hitting Nancy Chu in the face. Hard.

34

Immediately regretful of what he did, he wanted so badly to apologize but was caught up in his rage. His deep-set eyes literally curled up in his head like a Great White in a frenzy. Problem was, he'd just hit the most affluent family's child in the class—a child whose family owned a string of Chinese restaurants throughout Queens.

Needless to say, Mr. Hensland disappeared from the scene at school that week and we never saw him again. How he was able to get a job there in the first place, I'll never know. And even though I felt bad for him, I knew nobody with that kind of temper should be teaching 4th graders anywhere. But Daymond, for the next few weeks, was more jovial than usual, interacting with kids he'd never interacted with. I even saw him skip around the yard while playing, literally jumping up and clapping his feet together.

Though he couldn't have anticipated that string of events to take place, he sure did push the right buttons, and won. I often wondered if he was just that clever, and the incident, part of his plan.

To make matters worse, the movie, The Omen, was out and kids started calling him "Damien" in school and in the neighborhood. "I was called the devil all of my life," he would, many years later say in an interview with SmartCEO magazine from his office in the Empire State Building. He embraced it, never correcting anyone.

From that point on, I became increasingly concerned with what was going on with my friend, and after my own juvenile-like investigation, I finally found out. Though I didn't understand the depths of how this condition affects a child until many years later, I watched it unfold

35

in him firsthand. Daymond was suffering from the hurt of divorced parents, and from the melancholic anguish he felt from seeing the two people he loved most in life break up. On one hand he was angry with his father who had virtually disappear, and on the other hand he began resenting his mother for his feelings of abandonment. As a result, he began acting out and letting the world know how he felt. No one knew it was really a plea for help.

CHAPTER NINE
Birth of a Brander

It had only been a few years since Hip-Hop had come on the scene and began to grab the hearts and minds of youth with vividly descriptive lyrics that described a lifestyle we could relate to.

It was only a year or so prior that Daymond and I stumbled into our classmate Richard Pena's basement and heard "Rapper's Delight" for the first time. What was this, that commanded our attention so raptly and would change our lives forever? The music, the rapping, the break-dancing, the graffiti... we embraced every facet of this new subculture. It was ours. Something we felt we owned.

We had formed our crew and been listening to the music and watching the styles of dance everywhere we could but now our attention began to focus on what was perceived to be the more negative component of it—the graffiti.

Surrounded by spray-painted art everywhere in our community from its walls and trains, to even its public transportation, we admired the tagged names and colorful works of neighborhood artists who would paint the schoolyard handball courts we played in. To the average working citizen, it was perfectly understandable to see graffiti-riddled walls as vandalism. As a store owner, who wouldn't be angered by someone having spray-painted your storefront gates?

To us though, it was art. It was a way to have your voice heard, your style seen, a way to express how you felt inside, as well as a way to gain respect. One almost cannot put into words the feeling of walking into a park in broad day and seeing a huge piece of colorful art with animals, B-boy characters and wizards, all surrounding a strikingly beautiful laid out name. As observers in a museum sit down in front of masterpieces that speaks volumes to them, we would sit on the park bench for hours and watch handball players smack the ball against stunning hieroglyphic-like letters bursting with colors in a code that only we could understand. And to think of the planning that went into it was equally astounding.

The gathering of supplies, traveling with ladders and stools, painting with virtually no light in the dark, having to be quiet, and having limited time to do it in. Then if you were painting a more elaborate piece in a more conspicuous area with lots of traffic, the respect level for you went through the roof from your peers, as it was innately understood that, to do this, took heart. And lots of it.

These huge, colorful murals we speak of were called "Burners," and the more sophisticated street-wise artists took their talents to subway trains where their billboard canvases could be seen riding through the city on the metal clunks. If we had money to advertise on billboards I

38

imagine some of us would have, but most of these kids were dirt poor. Yet, they insisted their names, work, and voices be heard.

Fifteen years later, the child, Daymond, would become known as one of the world's premier branding experts. But this branding knowledge wasn't birthed in America's schools of higher learning, nor was hundreds of thousands of dollars invested in him to go to the top business academies available. His knowledge and insight into the power of branding came through the misty nozzle of a brightly-colored can of Krylon and homemade magic marker...graffiti!

CHAPTER TEN
Bombing Gone Bad

There were three artists in our area, all very bold and talented called "2D" (which stood for "Too Deadly"), "Demo," and "Quik," who displayed their works everywhere throughout our neighborhood. You couldn't escape seeing their work posted up somewhere in a single day and their names and styles became a part of our landscape. The abundant work of these artists and their choices of "advertising spaces" done in the night, created an aura of mysteriousness that made these artists cultural icons to us. To add to the effect, they were unknown or unseen by any of us.

Even in the alleyway of our school, by the time a school dance was over, we were released out the side door into the face of a huge, freshly painted, metallic silver "Demo" piece, still dripping wet. The nuns were stunned and appalled, but we were in awe.

Heavily influenced by two of these artists, Daymond and I paid homage by being little versions of these giants. Daymond was "2V" (which stood for "Too Vicious") and because I loved Demo's style of the letter "D," I named myself after the villain of my favorite comic book hero, "Dr.

Doom." Sammy's name was "Zoid." We became known as a trio. Where you saw one's name, you likely saw the others.

Before we had heart enough to tag on the streets, we spent days and days of school class time practicing and doodling in our notebooks, perfecting our craft. Like baby cubs learning how to play fight, we practiced our skills with pencils in the huge closet where we hung our coats. The teachers never paid it any attention, but the students seemed to like it. We, too, tried to portray ourselves as low-key and unknown, and the comments we heard were always positive.

Confidence now growing, we started bringing markers to schools and tagging up the bathroom stalls. Then from stalls to walls, and our notoriety grew more. We were becoming the school's bad boys and were loving the brand. The girls were too. We were now running neck-and-neck with the cool and bad-boy persona of Don Cotton. But bad-boy persona was about to get taken to another level by Daymond who was dealing with serious issues and not portraying to be a bad-boy.

Devising a plan to get the ultimate fame, after a few test runs of tagging the walls with spray-paint in the area, he wanted to tag up the outside of the school. His mother was away for the night, so I asked my father to spend that Saturday night over his house, as this was our only opportunity to ever get out late enough to do some real bombing (which is what graffiti artists call a spray-painting expedition).

As planned, about 2am, the latest we'd ever been out in our lives, we tagged up the front, the sides, and the door of our school with bright silver paint on the red bricks so everybody could see it Monday morning when we arrived.

42

Problem was, we hadn't thought it all the way through. We forgot that our school was the community's local Catholic church, and in seven hours scores of families would be headed there for Sunday mass. School was a day away. We started feeling guilty for what we did, as we now defiled a House of God, instead of our god-forsaken school, and began experiencing a crisis of conscience.

"You got any cleaner?" I asked in his room, totally guilt-ridden.

"Yeah, Carbona. It cleans anything," and we shot downstairs and pulled the bottle out from under the sink. "Half bottle, but it should do the trick."

We tested it out on the paint residue on our hands and it wiped right off. We looked at each other, grabbed some rags and shot out the door, racing back up to the school before it got light outside. Approaching morning time now, more traffic was rolling by.

When the cars passed and the coast was clear, we went to work scrubbing the wall with the cleaner. Problem was, we had spray-painted on bricks and the cleaner wasn't strong enough to penetrate its texture, so after scrubbing even harder and running out of cleaner, with no success we retreated back to the hideout, waiting for God to strike us dead. We sat there in his room miserable and quiet, just looking at each other.

Whoever said criminals always return back to the scene of the crime never lied, because four hours later, completely exhausted and having cleaned ourselves up and ironed our clothes, like two innocent 10-year old altar boys, we

43

dragged ourselves to Mass. When we turned the corner and expected the crime-scene tape and police around the school, we witnessed a miracle. To our relief, however, Sam, the trusted school custodian who lived in the basement of the premises, had gotten up and scrubbed most of the graffiti off in time for services.

We played it cool, went inside, prayed for forgiveness, seriously, and went home and slept for what seemed like days.

Five hours later, I was awakened by a shaken Daymond who'd been having a recurring dream for over a year about an Asian man. In this dream, he kept saying an Asian man was after him, chasing him. Odd thing about it, the man was chasing him to help him.

"What do you mean, chasing you to help? Why don't you just stop?" I'd ask.

"I can't," he'd always say. "I'm not ready." Little did he know, this was more than a dream, but a premonition years into the future of what was to come when he decided to change and get his life right.

Early Monday morning as I entered the school door late from being up half the night, I was greeted in the narthex by a lone Sister Helen, who I guess had pegged me as one of the suspects that vandalized the school over the weekend.

"Open your bookbag," she ordered, then helped me along by reaching in my bookbag herself. She carefully inspected the inside covers and its pages for any "Dr. Dooms'" or "2V's," but I was one step ahead as all she saw were great notes and clean sheets. I was up late transferring notes from my old graffiti-riddled notebook to a clean, crispy one.

Unable to find any convicting evidence, she sent me to her office where Daymond was already sitting. He was smart enough to never write graffiti in his, so he had nothing to worry about, but somehow Sister Helen was onto us.

While she left us under the supervision of her secretary, she went into her chambers for deliberations and I began sweating, thinking she was going to call my father who would of killed me if he'd found out what I'd done. Killed! But Daymond didn't seem to care, so I fed off his calm spirit and held my head.

Thirty minutes or so later, with no incriminating evidence, Sister Helen emerged from her inner office and directed us back to class. We had beat the case. But now we had a new problem. We had to change our names, leaving our old brands behind.

All the risk we took bombing, all the months of practice on those letters, and all the work we put into building up the respect and notoriety we gained from posting our names everywhere in our hood, was now out the window, just like that. Kaputz! This was a huge branding lesson learned, and feeling the emotional drain of losing what we built had affected us both. We felt empty, like we let our fans down, people who liked us, who believed in us, and we had no-one else to blame but us—certainly something a CEO would never want to put his company, customers, or employers through from doing something stupid. So we started again and built our companies up from scratch, with the now new names of "Tick" and Krak Five." It was here that we learned

45

one of the powerful lessons of Branding, backwards.

A school pic around third grade, looking like an up-and-coming pastor

Dee sharp as a tack

Outside our Queens famous, St. Gerard Majella school that Dee and I attended...
and bombed

Me (top left), Sammy (Zoid One), and guess who in the front row

Ms. John as beautiful as ever!

Lots of love in the John household!

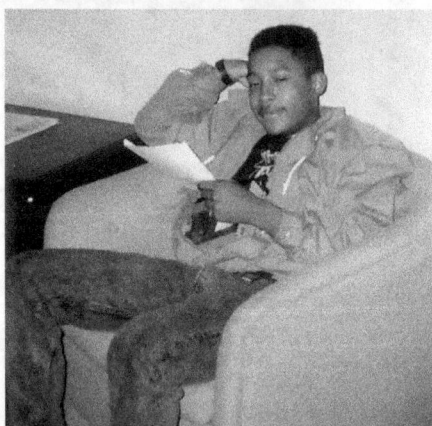

Dee practicing up for future business deals

Daymond (left), Me (middle), and Shameek again with
Daymond's nemesis teacher, Mr. Hensland

Dee with Terminator X

Still got his touch with the ladies!

Ms. John and Teddy after his time served

A neighborhood artist we looked up to around the St. Gerard area

Daymond's childhood sweetheart, Stacy (third from right) at her graduation

Chillin after church by 40 Projects in Southside, Queens

The throw-up I would become known for statewide; Krak 5,
the original Flinstone letters

FUBU—the idea sparked

Being appointed as an Ambassador by then-president Obama

Mom and son— still tight as can ever be!

CHAPTER ELEVEN
Fear Of Mom

Over the next few months Daymond, Sammy, and I worked super-hard to improve our drawing skills. Sammy was already a skilled artist, with books upon books of comic characters he'd drawn and created. We were all growing and getting better artistically, but Daymond's interest turned more towards girls, and his grades got worse.

Was he trying to emulate his father whose womanizing broke up the family? Not only were his actions mirroring that, but he was becoming more and more rebellious. He began doing things like stealing pencils, then comic books, then candy, then sodas, then bigger things like full-blown cakes in his coat and walking out the store when he had the money. It was as if he was trying to get caught, but he was too good.

I later learned from a counselor, who I was sent to because of my parent's divorce, that children who go through things like this experience trauma and begin acting out in different ways. Some change their eating habits, some throw tantrums and resist discipline, others get rebellious, start stealing, and/or regress in school. Daymond's symptoms ranged among the latter few and he kept stepping it up to get more attention—attention he wanted...or perhaps needed.

One Friday after school, we planned out a bike riding expedition for early the next morning and decided to ride further than we'd ever ridden before, even past Laces Roller Skating Rink deep in Long Island. We frequented the rink many times in the past when one of our parents would drive us. And the next morning, with our water bottles full and mounted on our bikes, we set out on the day-long journey. As an added amenity, it was almost second nature to carry our magic markers with us in case an opportunity to tag our names somewhere presented itself.

The plan was, as usual, to get lost, then find our way back. Well, we got lost alright, and found ourselves emerging far down Hillside Avenue by a public high school we'd heard about for years, Martin Van Buren.

After riding around and taking a tour of the school grounds, seeing as though it was Saturday and pretty much deserted, we rode up to the front doors ready to thrust our names into the psyches of street kids, whose respect we'd now gain.

As I pulled my homemade marker out and looked to the left into a dark classroom window, I saw a hanging flower pot slightly swinging. I thought it might've been the wind. When I opened the marker to begin, I looked back and the pot was sitting perfectly still. Daymond had already begun tagging his new name everywhere in the prime spaces, so I started writing too.

Moments later, detectives skidded up and had us halfway cornered. I tried to use my bike as a shield between me and one detective, and tried to shake and bake him to get away. In the midst of my razzle-dazzle, I looked over at Daymond who was just standing there with the detective, both of them looking at me. I couldn't understand why he had not made an effort to escape, as he was positioned better than me to get away.

When the officer nabbed me, the school principal and two cleaning ladies came out.

"That's him!" the one lady bellowed, pointing at me, obviously the one who stopped the flower pot from moving.

"Let's call their parents," the principle said, and when he did I pleaded with the man not to call my father. He must have thought my father would actually kill me the way I acted because he told the detectives to let me go. They were hesitant, but agreed, and took Daymond in the school to call his mother. Not a word was uttered from Daymond's lips. I sped away.

Fresh out of trouble just days after that, him, Sammy and I were walking by some factories and an 18-wheeler was double-parked outside of one waiting to go in. I knew what was on their mind when they stopped and looked from side to side, so I walked fast to get away from both of them. It was still daylight outside and it was a busy street. Sure enough, they spray-painted their names on the side of this man's new, clean white truck.

"Hey! Get over here!" the man shouted, bolting out of the factory yard after them, who were both a good ways behind me. I took off running, crossing Jamaica Avenue, zipping by the car wash and ran inside our friend Richard Pena's side door into his house, who was there in the kitchen about to eat dinner with his family.

Shocked that I would just open their door and walk in, they were even more shocked when Daymond and Sammy bursted in and ran into the basement with the man on their trail. The family, in shock from what was going on, just watched as the trucker walked Daymond out the house, hoisted up by his jacket collar.

"Dee!" I yelled as he walked by, indicating that he should hit the backyard once outside. But he ignored me and took his actions like a man, not uttering a word or thinking twice about involving Sammy or me in his capture. I was amazed by his courage.

The back-to-back incidences crushed Ms. John and Daymond watched as she cried for hours from the hurt he was causing. It was one incident after the next in their home, but she understood, on another level, why her son was acting out. He was hurting. And because he was unable to articulate the emotional trauma he was experiencing to his mother or father communicatively, he did so through his mischievous deeds. Though negative, he was now getting the attention he so badly wanted. Lots of attention from his mother, and a call or two from his father.

What he hadn't anticipated in it all was how badly he was hurting her—creating the same hurt for her that he saw his father do. And Daymond loved his mother too much for that. Through it all, she resolved to love him more.

CHAPTER TWELVE
Downward Spiral

The momentum of his downward spiral was already in full effect, and as his grades declined from D's, to now F's, he stopped doing his work now altogether. At a school meeting, where I happened to be present, they told his mother he had one more chance to pass an exam or he'd be kicked out. Whatever he was doing I demanded he stop and get serious about his work. I knew Sister Helen didn't like him and really preferred he be gone, and he was falling right into her trap.

"Dee, c'mon. Are you studying for the test tomorrow? It's easy," I told him that night over the phone, pleading with my friend who'd be heading to another school.

"I got it," he said, but he wasn't referring to study. He had his mind made up. Our paths were about to split ways.

Two weeks later, Sister Helen got what she wanted and gave Daymond his walking papers. And out of several schools in the area he could have chosen, he chose the toughest, a nearby intermediate school called I.S. 238. It had a terrible reputation. I was worried about him for weeks and grieved his absence for months as the school, for me, was never the same. I began to resent the nuns, who I remember seeing talk to him and his mother about the ultimatum. I couldn't comprehend that it wasn't their fault. Didn't they understand or have sympathy for what he was going through? But little did I know, Daymond was more in control of his ship than everyone thought.

Sometimes true warriors thrust themselves into the heart of what they fear, to look that fear in the face, then overcome it. This would be a distinguishing trait that the young man would show time and time again, to face his fears and embrace adversity, a characteristic of many successful men and women whose lives fly at high altitudes.

We either live our fears, or we live our dreams. The courageous life.

OUR SEPARATION over the next year had put some distance in the relationship, but we still got together from time to time to hang out.

When I'd stop by the house, he'd show me his photo album filled with new girlfriends, and as always, he had great taste! What amazed me the most was how he convinced them to pose nude. I was very proud of my boy's newfound artistic endeavor as a photographer, but I thought, Man he must have boss game!

His persuasive abilities became more and more apparent every time we'd chill out together. His mind was a gift.

58

CHAPTER THIRTEEN
Window Washing

Knowing I had a thing for business ventures like he did, he exercised his skills on me by trying to convince me that we could make tons of money washing car windows in traffic. I knew he was exaggerating about the money "his friends" were making off it, but I knew what he said was credible because every time my father and I would exit a tunnel into another borough, the homeless fellas would walk right up to your car and clean the windshield without you even asking. It was like, once they did it, you were obligated to give them a buck or two. Daymond's proposition sounded somewhat equivalent to selling someone a bridge, with this being the kid-version, but I kept listening.

I told him he was crazy, but he kept resorting back to his staple selling point, "his friends" were getting paid! Normally, I knew all his friends because they were my friends, but being as though he was going to a new school now with kids that were a lot bolder, his spiel was sort of credible. "Except we won't do it at the bridges and tunnels," he said. "We're going where the rich people are."

"Where's that?"

"Over there by Central Park, off Park Avenue in Manhattan."

I knew I was too shy to try this in major traffic like these other guys, but a little side street was a bit more in the realm of possibility for me. Plus, this calmed my fear of embarrassment in case somebody I knew saw me in the bridge scenario.

"When you talkin' 'bout?" I inquired, skeptically.

"Next week. I'll get the squeegee and bucket from my friends."

...This guy.

The anticipation of us having a knot full of dollars and a jarful of change at the end of the day motivated me the whole week, except I didn't listen close enough. He said "squeegee and bucket"...singular.

As we made our way up to 72nd Street and Central Park, we settled on this one-way street a block over. We sat there for about 30 minutes just watching the area, looking for anyone who might not like the idea of us peddling the rich, and the timing of the stoplight. Our attention was drawn away momentarily by John Madden who walked by like a regular person and went in his building. Our hopes for brighter days were up.

"Whassup?" asked Daymond, and as usual I summonsed up my nerves, grabbed the squeegee out the bucket and dove headfirst into the street. I tried to be bold and walk up to the cars like the other guys and put the squeegee on the windshield, but the look I saw on people's eyes as they locked their doors made me feel like crap. Then many of them turned their windshield wipers on long before I made it to their car, which I quickly learned meant, Stay away!

These people's windshields were filthy and I couldn't understand why they didn't want me to clean them. Maybe I wasn't scruffy-looking enough. Having a fresh haircut probably didn't help either.

Overwhelmed with rejection, I began to feel totally degraded, that is, until one old lady smiled as I approached her Mercedes at the red light. After cleaning her filthy windshield thoroughly, I smiled back, happy that I had gotten a customer. She cracked her window just a bit, and with the most generous nod handed me a shiny quarter like, Good job! Even being a teenager, I knew my self-worth was more than that, and that was the first time I ever felt really humiliated. Ready now to crawl under a rock somewhere and hide, I realized, *Where the hell is Daymond?*

He had been watching the whole thing from across the street and immediately conceded, "Let's get out of here."

Many years later I found out through my work in ministry that my leadership style was that of leading from the front, taking initiative. But back then I didn't know how he pulled off getting me out there alone as the test dummy. To his credit though, he was very persuasive—a leadership quality easy for a parent to overlook. If one discovers it, however, it is surely a quality that should be developed. Debate classes, Sales courses, church leadership, law, or reading books by Napoleon Hill should be encouraged. Who knows, your child could be our next great military leader, politician, lawyer, Chief Executive Officer, Director of a non-profit, or who knows, president.

There is a growing phenomenon showing up in studies of successful people in the world that suggests the D students usually become the most financially successful students. How could this be so?

How could someone like Oprah Winfrey, with a meager education who came from humble beginnings form such a conglomerate as she has today, while others born into privilege find themselves skimping through life?

Berk Hedges says in his book, *YOU Inc.*: "The A students become law professors. The B students become judges. And the C students make money working for the D students."

Research shows that only 20% of our success in life is attributed to IQ (Intellectual Intelligence), which A students rank among the highest. The other 80% of what we achieve is connected to our Emotional Intelligence, and the striking difference between the two is that, unlike IQ, EQ can be improved upon at any time of our lives. That being the case, if we improve our habits, embetter our character and learn the skills necessary to increase our market value, we can control our achievements. By changing the way we think and behave, we can change our circumstances. That's EQ. In other words, we're not talking about kids that have magical powers, but kids who have parents who spot talents and glimpses of greatness, and harness them.

CHAPTER FOURTEEN
The Slow Grind

Wisdom aside, my feelings had been jaded by the humiliation I'd felt from Daymond's bright idea and the fact that he chickened out and didn't hit the streets with me. So, as kids can sometimes be cruel, I made jokes about his teeth.

When he laughed, his smile revealed two extra teeth, the Canines, on top of the ones he had. I knew he had a complex about them, so in a one-on-one ranking session in his kitchen, with a healthy dose of meanness, I called him Dracula. Then I made a song about his photography and teased, "I vaunt to take your peekcha. I vaunt to take your peekcha."

I knew I'd struck a nerve because even he busted out laughing, but that was the end to the joking session as he kindly told me, "It was getting late." But under the kind dismissal were concealed thoughts of revenge. Utilizing his creative powers for evil, over the next three months he tormented me by drumming up an imaginary bully that was out to kill me.

Expertly done, even down to creating the menacing name of "Bruno," he told me this big dude from "Woodhull," which was the closest thing to a project in our neighborhood, was after me for spray-painting over his name and trying to talk to his girl (whose name he never provided). I didn't know what girl he was talking about or where I crossed Bruno's name out, but both were in the realm of something I'd do, so I believed him.

One particular day, Daymond "spontaneously" came to my class at St. Gerard right at the end of the day "just to say what's up" to me and Sammy, but warned me that Bruno was out front ready to ambush me. Wasting no time, I grabbed my books and slipped out the back door. Then at a house party he got me again. This time, I escaped through a window in the house. Mind you, he did so every time with a straight face.

Finally, after he figured I'd paid enough, he laughed, revealing his fangs in full form and told me he'd made it all up. Even though the thought crossed my mind to choke him out right there on the spot, I was overwhelmed with relief that I wasn't being hunted anymore. Touche'.

FAMILIES IN ST. ALBANS were always supplementing their work income with some side gig or hustle to make ends meet. Aside from my father's maintenance business, he plowed snow in the wintertime by hooking his plough up to his jeep and clearing out parking lots for the local businesses. He loved news of snowstorms heading our way. To bring in a little extra income into the John home, Margo renovated the basement, installing a working shower and bathroom, and rented it out.

Having interviewed a few potential tenants, she decided to let Mr. Al, a dark-skinned, heavy-set gentleman with Jheri-curls, who drove his old Buick along the bus route in Hollis to the subway station at 179th Street and Hillside Avenue, in the house. He picked up folks at the bus stop going to work and did the same thing when they came home. Being a gentle giant, people loved to be picked up at the bus stops by him and others who drove the regular bus route because they didn't have to stand out in the cold or heat waiting all day or night for the bus. Plus, if you were a regular customer of Mr. Al's, if your house wasn't too far off from the bus route at night, he'd drop you at your doorstep at no additional costs. This was especially popular with the ladies.

Rush hours were packed with folks exiting the subways at night looking for drivers, and Mr. Al was out there, rain, sleet, or snow.

At the end of each shift when the rush hour subsided, he would often go to his basement apartment for a nap, but sometimes would come upstairs to the kitchen and let Daymond help wrap the jars of coins he had. This was a task Daymond loved, especially since his payment for help would be the odd coins out.

It was from Mr. Al that Daymond learned the importance and value of nickels and dimes, who would eventually mature into dollar bills. The slow grind. The beauty of this style of business resonated with him because of a lesson Ms. Gallagher taught us in 3rd grade.

65

She said around 1849, droves of people headed out west to California, Nevada, Colorado and Montana in search of gold. Stories had circulated that miners were out there striking it rich, so many families packed their wagons up and headed out. Thing was, seldom did people ever strike it rich from gold mining. But there was a fella whose business consistently made him rich. The Hardware Store owner. The folks who sold tools to the miners; the shovels, picks, pans, and axes. Though it might have took them longer, their sales were consistent and their growth was steady.

A year or so later, after Mr. Al found him a bigger place elsewhere, Daymond talked his mother into driving the route in her old, but clean, Grand Marquis. And Daymond sometimes rode shotgun for protection. I remember exiting the subway in a snowstorm one day and seeing Ms. John outside directing passengers to her car. I thought, Now that's a trooper of a mom! I loved her for that! They had become a mother and son team on the grind. Years later, he would accumulate enough coins to quit his job as waiter, buy a full-sized Econoline Van, and register himself as a legitimate Livery Service driver, licensed and insured. But Mr. Al wasn't the only business mentor Daymond had in his life.

With not much of a relationship with his father since the divorce at 10, Ms. John knew the importance of having good male role models in her son's life. She began letting a financial advisor friend she knew start coming to the house for tea or dinner. The mild-mannered, middle-aged man with dirty blonde hair, blue eyes and tanned skin, would often come by and share his experiences on what it was to be a man, as well as some nuggets about the business world. The man saw something special in Daymond and would remain in his life to this day, having believed in him as one of the first investors of his clothing empire.

Having mentors in one's life is absolutely crucial to one's success. They believe in our potential and help direct our lives in the right direction. With the right mentor, one can learn the lessons of a profession in minutes that may take the average person years. If you don't have any in your life, find one.

CHAPTER FIFTEEN
The Team

The time had come for us to go to high school, and as fate would have it, we both went to high schools a few blocks away from each other. I went to Holy Cross High and Dee went to Bayside High, both way out in Bayside, Queens, an upper-middle-class neighborhood on the outskirts. We crossed paths less and less and began to create different circles of friends, but our common interests always brought us back together.

My father and I were planning a camping trip upstate so I invited Daymond for the weekend so we could get back to the good ole' times. He asked if a friend could come and I told him we might as well see if Sammy wanted to come too, who now called himself Shameek and was a member of the 5% Nation. This was a group that promoted black pride and taught that black people were gods. Daymond and I would make fun of him when he tried to sell us on his new group's views, because it was hard to see him as a tough "god-body" when we saw him as an altar-boy years earlier in school. But off we went camping like old times.

69

Daymond's new friend, Teddy, was fun to be around and listen to, especially since his voice was high-pitched like Mike Tyson's. He was from Baisley, a rough part of South Side Jamaica, Queens, where the notorious Supreme Team crew reigned. His tough neighborhood stories entertained us every night as we roasted marshmallows or ate barbeque chicken by the campfire.

As usual, Daymond and I were up every morning ready to hit the lake to do what we do, but we'd often wind up late because of our two lazy pals. On the lake, Teddy was like a fish out of water, the epitome of a "city boy," as he didn't know the first thing about fishing or being on a boat. He came out with us the first two days, but no more after that. I could tell he had his mind on something heavy and it wasn't until we went hiking that he opened up.

He was offered an opportunity to be a part of the Supreme Team gang with a starting lieutenant's position, as one of the captains was dating his sister. The Supreme Team had a longtime history of crime, violence, and drugs in Queens, and ran their organization like a real business, with an iron fist. He had to make his decision when we returned.

We all knew that taking this position would financially change his life, but we also knew they were dangerous guys. I'd personally had a run-in with them years earlier as a couple of friends and I were driving around and saw some girls running from some guys who were throwing bottles at them. My neighbor, who had just received an inheritance and bought a fancy Lincoln Towncar, pulled up beside them and asked them if they wanted a ride. Without hesitation, all three jumped in. It was three of us too.

70

They indicated they'd wanted to "hang out" and my horny friend whose car it was shot to the ATM. Unable to make a withdrawal on the peaceful Sunday afternoon for some reason, the girls suggested they knew where to get money from and had us park on a backstreet corner somewhere on the Southside. Thirty minutes passed, no girls, and I urged my boy to leave, but he ignored me. He had his mind set on hanging with the girls.

He decided to drive around the block looking for them, and as he did three guys walked out of a house, then stopped in their tracks as we cruised by slowly. Instead of leaving, my boy goes back to the parking spot and parks, where the girls finally came, jumped in, and told us to, "Go!"

We went to a Jamaican restaurant not far away. I chose to stay outside with the girl I was with.

Shortly thereafter, a car pulled up behind us and a short, light-skinned guy with green eyes emerged in an all-white Adidas suit and diamond studded medallion. He got out with another guy and indicated to his Kangol-wearing driver to, *Go get the sh*#*. The driver skidded off.

"Cat, get out the car," he calmly said, ordering the girl I was with to exit the vehicle. When she did, I went into the restaurant and told my boys the dudes we just saw come out of the house are outside, and we need to go. One of the girls looked out the window. "Oh sh*#, that's Prince!" Prince was Supreme's violent nephew who ran the organization while Supreme was locked up.

No sooner than we all hauled into the Lincoln did the other car pull up behind us. Skidding off through an abandoned gas station, we were engaged in a high-speed chase down Baisley Boulevard with these guys in hot pursuit, shooting at us. Everyone slumped, Kangol managed to pull up beside us with his gun out the window about to shoot, when my boy slammed on the brakes. They skidded sideways in front of us in an effort to stop us by all means and they did. We crashed into their car, hitting them so hard that their car smacked into a turning bus, knocking it on two wheels.

Completely unrattled, the men got out with guns drawn. When they got out so did I. Being trapped in a car wasn't a good look.

"Get back in the car!" one barked.

"No sir!" I told him as I took off and jumped through a nearby ground-level apartment building window. You know ya' boy don't stick around!

The lady inside nodded to the direction of her front door which I opened and was unfortunately greeted by one of the henchmen, who grabbed me by the back of my neck, drug me to their car, and threw me in the backseat with him. Kangol and Prince were in the front.

"To the spot," the green-eyed leader ordered in the front, whose instructions had Kangol zipping through the small one-way streets of Queens at top speeds. "Slow down," he said with a wave of his hand, and immediately he eased up on the accelerator. This was absolutely their hood, and Prince absolutely their leader.

With a gun in the lap of the henchmen beside me, Prince began questioning me about the girls, which I made crystal clear we'd just met. "We were trying to have a good time," I told him, truthfully. Then we turned slowly onto a street with no houses that said, Dead End, which to me took on a relevance far beyond what the sign had originally intended.

As we pulled around a bin, I saw the tail-end of the gold Lincoln parked.

"Your stories better match," Prince said as he got out and walked toward the Lincoln. And by the grace of God they did. Shortly thereafter, the green-eyed boss nodded back to the henchman to let me go and I wasted no time scurrying away. They thought the girls were using us to try to rob them.

"These are like, serious dudes," I explained to Teddy about the kind of individuals he was thinking about working with. "This Prince is the same dude you're talking about."

Daymond agreed and told him it was a terrible idea, and that there were other ways to make money. But Teddy kept telling us the problems he was having at home and the reasons why he should.

Later that night, we talked about it again, and though he said he understood where we were coming from, he explained that his risks in the operation were going to be minimal. Though it wouldn't be the last time we talked about it over the weekend, it was the last time for Daymond.

While he and I walked into town the next day, I asked him why he didn't try to talk some sense into Teddy.

"He's got his mind made up," he said. Then he told me

his mother's friend, Steve, told him something he never forgot. He said when people come to his office for advice and he gives it to them, after the third time he hears them say, "Yeah, but..." he told Daymond he excuses them and gets back to his work. "Some people like to focus on their problems," Steve told him. "These are small-minded individuals who never came for advice in the first place, but just to waste your time." I shut my mouth right there.

I thought that was just the greatest wisdom ever and I realized right then the importance of mentors and wise counsel. Daymond had good professional people around him. Good influences.

As the months went by, Teddy started coming through in nice cars. He made his choice and started moving up in the ranks fast with the crew. He would often stop by Daymond's in something new, but at least had enough respect for Ms. John to park his new car up the street. He knew he wasn't living right.

Seeing the fruits of Teddy's endeavors, the cars, money, and jewelry up close and personal would be quite tempting to any young aspiring entrepreneur. Though Daymond valued the friendship he had with him, he wasn't a follower who would follow somebody just because of the things they had. In the midst of that, he still got a job at a popcorn stand and rose above the temptation to do wrong. He'd begun developing personal integrity—that quality of doing the right thing even when no-one was looking. He was far from perfect, but something was transforming inside him.

Even greater than that, his chief driving force for staying on track wasn't integrity, self-control, a good nature, or fear of

74

getting caught. It was the fear of his mother. Not in the sense that he feared her wrath if he got in trouble, but Daymond's greatest fear was letting his mom down. He couldn't stand to put his mother through that pain anymore.

CHAPTER SIXTEEN
Servant Leadership

Green Acres Mall, located in the well-to-do Valley Stream area that bordered Queens and Long Island, was a popular shopping haven for both counties and mixed races. Its huge multiplex cinema drew large crowds of people from all over Queens to watch movies. One of their premier attractions on the mall grounds was Red Lobster, a restaurant where Daymond scored a job.

The restaurant would get so busy in the evenings that families and couples would wait in its lounge and bar area for up to two hours before being seated. He loved the busyness and fast-moving pace of the restaurant business, especially on weekends, as that meant more tips for him as host or waiter.

Seeing another version of Mr. Al's slow-grind principle of watching coins turn into dollars, he'd become a believer that the Tortoise could win the race and saved portions of his tips daily.

One particular discipline that Daymond developed was the ability not to live above his means; one that he inherited from his mother who, at any time could have bought a new car or new home, but rathered keep her old green Marquis and fully pay off her existing mortgage.

He eventually saved up enough to buy a 15-year old, beat up Mustang hatchback to get back and forth to work. He wasn't interested in looks, but functionality. Now he could more efficiently use his time by driving from school to work, and on his day off, to an occasional club.

When we packed into the little white monster to go clubbing, he wouldn't dare spend his hard-earned money on high-priced drinks at the bar. He'd stop by the famous Pop & Kim's convenient store on Merrick Boulevard, who were known for carrying 40oz.'s of Olde English so cold that frost covered the bottles. The Chinese owners hired a neighborhood addict who was an absolute expert at mastering the art of freezing beer just enough so the bottle wouldn't break. Neighborhood tradition in our part of Queens was, before you went out to a party or club on the weekends, you stopped by Pop & Kim's first.

That tradition bode well with Daymond, as he figured it wiser to buy his drink beforehand rather than waste big bucks on drinks in the club. And being the responsible young man he was becoming, we all appreciated that he wouldn't drink until we made it to the club. By the time we made it to the parking lot, the ice inside would be melted, and the beer just cold enough to enjoy.

The Red Lobster job did more for him, however, than provide nice tips and a weekly check. Not only was it teaching him a humble servant leadership model which is the mark of the greatest of leaders, but he was on the front lines of learning the valuable people skills that would later help him understand the most vital parts to a business's success, like customer service, consumer behavior, and employee morale. Of equal importance, he learned how to take personal responsibility for his success.

He began to understand the simple principle of employing excellence over mediocrity. As an example, he would call respectable taxi drivers he knew, whose cars were clean and prices fair, for customers who needed a ride home from the restaurant. The customers appreciated that. In the summertime when he worked the slow, late-afternoon shift, he would also offer the businessmen at his tables crispy Wall Street Journals to read while they waited on their food.

Another valuable lesson he learned was that folks were not eating there necessarily for the food, but for the experience; a chance for romance, or an opportunity to spend quality time with their family or friends. It was a time of bonding for them, and if he could help make that experience a time they'd remember, they'd come back and request his tables. That, was Emotional Intelligence at its finest—taking practical steps to improve one's character or service. And that's what Daymond did. He understood that people don't necessarily remember what you say to them, but they will always remember how you made them feel.

To the average kid, working there was just a job. But to Daymond, this was leadership school with hands-on training.

79

CHAPTER SEVENTEEN
Frugality & Fairness

All the time, he never forgot the amounts of money he saw Mr. Al make by driving working folks to and from the subway station, and the supplemental income he and his mother made on the nights they drove the route. After two years of working and saving, Daymond was able to put a down-payment on his own slightly used van. Now he could nearly triple what he saw Mr. Al making! One problem though, he wasn't the only one with a van, and cutting into the Department of Transportation's market share at the time was bringing on lots of heat from the authorities.

Random stops were being made by the boys in blue, and massive tickets were written to drivers carrying passengers with no livery insurance. Getting smart, the van drivers formed a Livery Service corporation, under which the drivers became independent business owners who were now totally legitimized. As long as the State of New York was cut into the action through taxation, the State of New York backed off.

Despite Daymond being busy and things going very well

with the van business, he never was the all-work, no-play type. So as we were commonly accustomed to occasionally recreate and party, we headed for the strip club.

Now that we had a nice, roomy and reliable 15-passenger van to roll around in, we picked up all the homies and headed out to one we'd been trying to get to for years in New Jersey. It was a little raunchier and to our liking, as customers were permitted to touch the strippers, but we could never make the trip because we didn't have a vehicle reliable enough. That is, until now.

The first week we went, it was all good, girls everywhere and just what we hoped for. I mean, Daymond and I always had very similar tastes in women, nice looking, sweet, classy, with a good head on their shoulders. But we also had another side that inclined to the lower-end type. Weaves, contacts, bullet wounds, cheap lipstick and even cheaper perfume, was just fine with us, and The Country Inn embodied all of that.

The second week, however, went a little different. When everybody piled into the van, we rode to Pop & Kim's listening to the Red Alert radio show, jamming and feeling good in anticipation of the night ahead. While at the store, Daymond mentioned we ante up for gas money. He might as well have been talking to the sliding doors, because nobody responded. When everybody got their soda and beer, we pulled off and he mentioned again that everybody needed to send a couple of dollars up for gas. Two miles down the road with us rapping to songs on the radio and sharing neighborhood news with each other at a high decibel, we found ourselves parked on the side of the road. Finally, when everybody noticed we weren't moving anymore, the talking and rapping stopped and we all looked up at Daymond, who had parked and quietly cracked his 40oz still in the bag, and uncharacteristically started taking a few sips.

"What's going on?"

"What happened?" came mumbles from the back, wondering why we were stopped.

Daymond, patient and humble, was no pushover or one to be taken advantage of. Where the average young guy with a new business might've overlooked such a small thing and footed the bill, he felt that everybody should pay their fair share. He was a frugal young man, who had gained a healthy respect for a dollar and wasn't wasteful of a cent.

Though some grumbled about it and called him petty for years to come, it was this justice and fairness in his dealings, both to himself and others, that laid the foundation for him in the future to have a reputation as an honest and fair businessman—one who could be trusted—an absolute necessity for any businessman if he desires long-term success.

One could use deception to gain an advantage and short-term success in business, but in the end the fruits of his labor will be ruin. The wise businessman knows that justice balances everything out, so he, being fair-minded, will make sure he pays his just share in his dealings, and always compensates a man for his services. Likewise, he is not slack in requesting compensation for himself.

83

CHAPTER EIGHTEEN
Strength in Humility

While Run-D.M.C., the rap group from our neighboring town in Hollis, Queens, had solidly set their mark on the world of Hip-Hop, we had our emerging star from St. Albans who had begun to win the hearts of girls around the way by earnestly telling them in song, *he needed love*. L.L. Cool J was hitting the industry hard with hit after hit and becoming a national heartthrob across the nation. But in between time on the road and making records, he was on the block with us drinking 40's and chilling.

When he caught a big break and was invited to tour with Run-D.M.C. and the likes of Whodini and Public Enemy, DJ Cut Creator who lived on the next block over, and E-Love who lived directly across the street from me, invited us to any show we could make it to. So whenever the tour hit the surrounding states our whole crew would posse up and drive to the shows.

Once we hit the designated town, we'd get rooms at whatever hotel L.L. was staying and head to the concert where backstage passes would be issued to us. Anyone whose done tours knows that backstage passes meant power—power, because all the fans who want to be with the stars will do anything to get to them or around them, so with the pass, we played like we were important parts of the tour.

The good thing about L.L.'s performance was that, at some point of every show, he'd invite the females to the "After-party" at his hotel. And of course, by the time we got there, we were greeted by fans eager to get up to his floor. We had our pick of the litter with girls who wanted to hang out and would then, head on up. These events became one of the biggest pastimes for our crew for years to come.

Thing was, Daymond lived about a mile away from my house and wasn't from my immediate area, so he didn't have the close relationship that most of us did with L.L. or the entourage, but he would just enjoy himself and steadily build a rapport with the entertainers. It was during these times that I saw a level of strength not common in a 16-year old. Not the kind of macho strength that pushes people around or blows up on people, but strength exhibited in the ability to be himself, to be a kind and gentle leader amidst guys rough around the edges—a quality hard to maintain among street guys. All the other guys were trying to be someone they weren't and I saw right through it. But not Daymond. He always remained himself. This form of leadership would take him a long way in forging trusted relationships, and would be one to pay handsome dividends in the future. Had he not established a respected relationship with the 6'5" rapper from Farmers Boulevard, history might've turned out differently for the future branding mogul who later drove over to L.L.'s house and asked him to endorse his clothing line. When L.L. agreed and began wearing it on his sitcom TV show and commercials, no-one knew this simple relationship would reap such benefits and go on to change the fashion industry and hip-hop culture forever.

CHAPTER NINETEEN
Healing Through Adversity

One of the downsides in Daymond's leadership ability was that he didn't get along well with other young leaders of his stature.

A different graffiti artist friend of mine from a circle of my geeky art friends started coming around my neck of the woods to hang out with us. He began accompanying us to parties and strip clubs, and was an aspiring filmmaker going to college. We even went to a party or two on his school's campus.

This friend, Hype Williams, had recently landed a job as a gaffer for Classic Concepts, a burgeoning music video company making a big-budget name for itself in the industry with wild success. The company's owner, recognizing they had a brilliant young talent in their camp, began letting him shoot the extremely low-budget videos the company didn't have time to shoot. If they finished production early on a big video, they'd let him use the cameras and lighting equipment until they were due back the next day. Creating a buzz within the Hip-Hop community from his great work, he quickly became a hot item in the music industry.

Staying true to his low-budget sensibilities, he tagged along with us to clubs in search of talent and exotic dancers, not for the lap dances. His high-brow attitude didn't bide well with Daymond, and the two began to dislike each other, slamming car doors in each other's faces and frequently exchanging harsh words and insults.

Then I noticed this same attitude towards another associate of mine, a young DJ from Hollis who I'd started going to the studio with. This DJ, then known as DJ Irv, would come around our block trying to make a few bucks by selling his homemade mixtapes, but I began to notice friction between them two as well. This guy was nobody then, but years later went on to form one of Hip-Hop's most powerful record labels, Murder Inc. Daymond and Irv Gotti's dislike for each other even carried over into their mogul years, where street beefs began between camp members at a club, in which ya boy, being the common denominator, found myself attempting to mediate from prison. They both ended up backing down, thankfully, because both had hooligans ready to prove themselves, and both knew they were in dangerous waters with too much to lose.

I didn't fully comprehend what was going on then because we were all young men trying to find our way, but in retrospect I came to understand simply that Daymond didn't play well with other children...particularly young bosses—a quality that I later learned in life only comes with experience and maturity. But a quality, to his strength, he later learned to overcome, understanding that every great leader needs other great leaders around them if they are to achieve greatness.

90

The time for serious life decisions came when a crew of about twelve of us, this time including Carl and Alex, two friends that Daymond would later bring on board to start FUBU, decided to take a train ride to 42nd Street in Manhattan to have some fun. In these days, everything was happening on The Deuce and people would come from all over the city on weekends to walk up and down the street filled with flashing bright lights, musicians, dancers, hustlers, game rooms, peep shows, ladies of the night and every other manner of decadence New York had to offer. We just wanted to walk up and down the busy street and be where everything was happening.

On the subway ride there, our whole crew got drunk and began agitating people. The transit police took notice and began keeping a close eye on us. When we exited the train and it pulled off, a belligerent friend of ours shattered the train window right where the police were standing inside.

By the time we got to Times Square, the transit cops had notified the authorities above and not five minutes out of the subway station, we got swarmed on by the cavalry. Alex was slammed through the windshield of a police car in the foray, then arrested with the belligerent friend. Daymond took off, and I managed to meld into the crowd like a pedestrian and got away, but we were all in a frenzy and found ourselves scattered throughout the city. This run-in, which could have gone terribly bad with us being justifiably shot and killed by police, was way too serious and served as a wake-up call for Daymond. While he found himself scuffed up and filthy, hiding out between cars on a backstreet curb blocks away in front of a hole-in-the-wall bar, he realized that his life and freedom nearly being taken away wasn't the road he wanted to take. Though he wasn't particularly sure what he wanted to do with his life, one thing became clear—he didn't want to continue down this path.

Choosing the direction we want to go in life is often more important than success or any goal we want to reach and this moment became his crossroad. The wrong road was one he knew he didn't want to travel down, and for some, that's enough to be set on the right one.

On the lonely train ride home, with ripped jeans and scraped-up hands, he decided it was time to get serious and change his life.

Although he would still occasionally hang out together with friends, the partying times began to become far and few in-between. Most of our friends began to weed themselves out anyway by getting involved in more serious street-life activities. Never one to be judgmental, Daymond just chose to stand his ground as a man and focused on hard work with his van, distancing himself with the riff-raff.

When approached with opportunities to make quick cash, he politely, but firmly, stood on his convictions. This strength to refuse those pressures were often met with laughter and scoff, and thus, he was given the nickname by friends of *Leery Dee*, a new name he proudly embraced. To him, it signified caution, to which he began exercising with every decision.

Even though some would joke and started calling him square for choosing to take the straight path, they all respected him. Especially me, who watched it all and was silently proud to see my partner on the right track and standing firm on what was right. They didn't know him like I knew him or knew the challenges I saw him overcome. They didn't know the pain he caused his dear mother, and how he resolved like a man to never hurt her anymore. Lifting himself above the trauma of being abandoned by the most important man in his life and the resulting pettiness of doing wrong, integrity had found its way into the being of the young businessman and began to make him whole. Healing had made its rounds and found a home in the young man's heart.

CHAPTER TWENTY
Young Power Move

Daymond began reading books on his own and one of his favorites became, *Think and Grow Rich*, by Napoleon Hill. In the book, Hill states that "Every adversity has within it the seed of an equivalent or a greater benefit."

With every seed planted properly in good soil, while the roots grow downward into dark places attracting the earth's rich minerals to itself, equally, at the opposite end there is fruit that will burst forward from its stems into the sunlight of the sky.

The principle, at a low point in the young Daymond's life, set him on a path that would begin the sprouting of good fortune that would later go on to change the world.

The success of his clothing empire that would, at its early stages, gross him upward of $350 million in one year, didn't start immediately after the night he found himself on the dark Manhattan curb. His change of heart and mind solidified his choice to continue working hard and doing the right thing through whatever struggles may come, which was enough to help him stick it out through other menial jobs and unsuccessful side hustles.

Then one day, some years later, he decided to sell some winter hats his mother helped him sew together. But if he took those hats and attempted to sell them at the neighborhood corner or flea market, you might've never come to have known a clothing line named FUBU or an icon named Daymond John. But because he used the business principle he learned naturally as a child, he took those hats and began selling them directly across the street from his mother's old job at the nail salon on The Ave, The Beehive!

It was there, that the hats sold like hotcakes and it was there that an inspired Daymond rushed home to make more.

The rest of the story is the FUBU history you've all come to know and love...the story in the textbook!

EPILOGUE

As I sat outside the classroom watching the students through the window reading the Horatio Alger-like rags-to-riches story of this boy from Queens in the textbook, I could tell the story was inspiring them to believe that they could do it too.

What they didn't know was how the kid *Displayed Power* by choosing to sell the hats at that very Location on The Ave where his mother used to work. They couldn't know *The Brand Within* was being formed in the young man through the turmoil of emotions he had to overcome as a result of divorced parents; or of how he had to resist the powerful allure of fast cash in the streets illegally—one that so many young men and women fall victim to while trying to finance their dream. This story is never told. And they definitely wouldn't be able to comprehend the hunger of the freezing wolf who bonds with other like-minded wolves around him to find food, then clean the bone, even chewing the gristle, making sure he uses whatever means and resources he has at his disposal to make something happen in this cold world—*The Power of Broke*.

That's what he did when he got with like-minded buddies

and started FUBU. That's what he used when he needed a logo. He put his slippers on and walked up the street to Sammy's house to ask him to "draw one right quick"—the same "FB" logo you saw displayed on MTV, BET, and across the chest of L.L., other world-famous rappers, and kids in neighborhoods throughout the world; Africa, Russia, Italy, Japan, Brazil and more. The power one has when one uses the resources at his disposal to the max, which is really all one needs...if he only knew it.

You all know the story from here, from the hats on, to how he gained momentum with the clothing line and had to take a second mortgage out on him and his mother's house. Then needing investors and distributors, to amazingly meeting up with the Asian man from his dreams who finally hunted him down once his heart was ready. This Asian man, who came in the form of a company named Samsung, who stepped in and helped Daymond generate over $5 billion worldwide to date.

You don't, however, know the story of Teddy, who while FUBU was on the rise in the 90's, found himself on the run and facing life in prison because of his association with Prince, who is now serving Life himself. Or the story of those who teased him on the van; three dead, two strung out on drugs, four in prison, and one working. Or me, whose story I hesitate to mention but am sure you're wondering about. I won't do you like that. They called me Al Monday, that was my rap name, a name I inherited from an older street legend in Detroit. I started making hot music with Irv and my team was forming. Any success was going toward the vision, which was to bring all the young talent I was surrounded with under one multi-media conglomerate roof—clothes, music, and film. I knew what I had, but my impatience, zeal, and boldness once again caused me to jump out at a stupid opportunity to make the seed money necessary to make the vision happen. Who in the next thirty quick days found himself facing charges for the murder of someone I never met or knew. A movie you'd never want to live in (google for story). But this is not about me.

This is a story about a guy who, when he became successful, took all of my elderly father's bills and paid all his debts. About a guy who, despite possibly smearing his own reputation, stood by his boy facing serious charges and told the judge I didn't do it. This is the story about real leadership—and a real friend.

So I end here where the success story begins—with the hats. And in the spirit of them, my man, I tip mines to you, for being an OVERCOMER. I understand now that success is relative to one's values, and that one must sometimes fail in one direction, so that success may be found in another. That, for me, has been empowering others through works like this and ministry, one in which I am called to intercede. Until my hour comes, take comfort in knowing you have a warrior holding you down, covering you in heavy prayer against the hearts of small-minded people who may seek to hurt or harm you.

I love you bro, from the bottom of my heart, and hope the world can benefit from these glimpses of your childhood genius!

99

About The Author

Alfred Cleveland is a visionary from Queens, New York, and a graduate of *The Urban Ministry Institute (T.U.M.I.)*.

He co-founded the *Young Christian Professionals (Y.C.P.)* with his partners, and the *Y.O.U.R. Relationship* Program for couples enduring incarceration, with his wife of 21 years, Roberta.

He is also an outstanding artist who loves to write screenplays, music and poetry. His latest EP, "Welcome Back" (Deacon Cleveland) can be found on most major streaming platforms.

His other books are *Diamond Bullets: 44 Laws Dispelling Illusions of the Game (Al Monday)*, and *3 Strands, 1 Cord: A Couple's Guide to Understanding Incarceration.*